CAKES
for Romantic Occasions

MAY CLEE-CADMAN
of *Maisie Fantaisie*

D&C
David and Charles

www.rucraft.co.uk

A DAVID & CHARLES BOOK
Copyright © David & Charles Limited 2009, 2010

David & Charles is an F+W Media, Inc. company
4700 East Galbraith Road
Cincinnati, OH 45236

First published in the UK in 2009
Reprinted in 2010
This paperback edition first published in the UK in 2010

Text and designs copyright © May Clee-Cadman 2009, 2010
Photography © David & Charles 2009, 2010

A catalogue record for this book is available from the British Library.

ISBN-13: 978-0-7153-3176-7 hardback
ISBN-10: 0-7153-3176-0 hardback

ISBN-13: 978-0-7153-3154-5 paperback
ISBN-10: 0-7153-3154-X paperback

Printed in China by RR Donnelley
for David & Charles
Brunel House   Newton Abbot   Devon

Commissioning Editor: Jennifer Fox-Proverbs
Editor: Bethany Dymond
Assistant Editor: Kate Nicholson
Project Editor: Ame Verso
Art Editor: Sarah Clark
Designers: Sabine Eulau and Victoria Marks
Art Direction: Sarah Underhill
Production Controllers: Kelly Smith
Photographer: Ginette Chapman

David & Charles publish high quality books on a wide range of subjects.
For more great book ideas visit: **www.rucraft.co.uk**

Contents

Sweet Nothings

Look of Love

Young Love

Introduction

I am delighted to introduce you to my second cake-decorating book, which is a collection of designs dedicated to the subject of love. In my first book, *Sweet and Simple Party Cakes* (D&C, 2008), I looked at my cake portfolio and picked out some of my favourite designs to give you an idea of the cakes that I had been making at Maisie Fantaisie since the company was established in 2003. This time, rather than taking cakes from my portfolio, I decided that the book should be full of brand new designs and fresh inspiration.

As I hope you will be able to see from the pages that follow, I have had a lot of fun putting this book together! I have taken inspiration from all sorts of things: the garden (Forget-me-not, page 40), clothes designs (Summer Sun, page 46), jewellery (Shooting Star, page 68), ceramic designs (Butterfly Bliss, page 74) and interiors (Ivory Swag, page 80) among many other sources.

The book has been broken into three chapters each with slightly different styles. The first chapter, Sweet Nothings, is about fun love. The second chapter, Look of Love, focuses more on traditional wedding cake designs, and the third chapter, Young Love, looks to engagements and valentines for inspiration. Each cake is complemented by a cookie, cupcake or mini cake design, as these sweet little treats are impossible to resist. The instructions for the cakes in this book are here to guide you, but there is no reason why you can't use them as a springboard for your own ideas, adapting any designs to suit your particular occasion.

I really hope you enjoy making these cakes as much I have enjoyed creating the book.

Happy baking!

May Clee-Cadman

You can't beat the wonderful smell of fresh baking and the satisfaction you feel when your cake rises to perfection.

How to Use this Book

Over the next few pages you will find a guide to the cake-making techniques you need to create the designs in the book. This covers:

Cake-making equipment – both essentials and more specialist items you may not need every time

Four delicious traditional cake recipes

Different types of icing and fillings, and how to work with them

Putting a cake together – icing the board, levelling a cake and assembling tiers with dowels

How to make and ice cupcakes, mini cakes and cookies

The following chapters will guide you through the processes involved for successful cake making. Whether you are an experienced baker or a first-timer, you will find recipes and designs that suit every occasion. Easy-to-follow step instructions and sumptuous pictures will help you to create beautiful and delicious cakes for all your friends and family to indulge in. Why not be creative and adapt any of the designs to suit a particular occasion or theme? Above all, enjoy yourself!

Techniques

Equipment

Here is the complete list of all the cake-making equipment used for the designs in the book, but you will not need everything every time. Check the materials and equipment lists at the beginning of each chapter for the specific tools required.

1 **Greaseproof paper** To line the cake tins.

2 **Spirit level** To ensure that stacked cakes are level.

3 **Large and small palette knives** For smoothing buttercream and jam onto cakes.

4 **Pastry brush** For brushing water onto under iced cakes.

5 **Large rolling pin** For rolling out the sugarpaste cake coverings.

6 **Small rolling pin** For rolling out the flowerpaste and icing for the sugarcraft details.

7 **Icing smoother** For achieving a really smooth icing finish.

8 **Small plastic board** To roll out flowerpaste and icing for the sugarcraft details.

9 **Cocktail sticks** For applying food colourings to sugarpaste icing.

10 **Flower foam pad** Also called a celpad. Used to thin and curl the flowerpaste.

11 **Cake boards** Drum and thin hardboard, various sizes, round (see individual projects for specific size required).

12 **Plastic dowels** Used to support tiered cakes.

13 **Paintbrushes** A range of sizes for painting, dusting and dabbing.

14 **PME1 bone tool** Used with the flower foam pad to form and curl flower petals.

15 **Cutters** Small leaf; rose leaf; small blossom plunger; large and small butterfly; large and small flower; large, medium and small daisy; various round; large and small star; large and small rose petal; large and small heart plunger; small primrose; small heart.

16 **PME piping nozzles** No.1.5, No.2, No.3, leaf, savoy star.

17 **Tilting turntable** For use when a cake is being decorated.

18 **Stay-fresh plastic mat** To cover up flowerpaste to stop it drying out.

19 **White stamens** For flower centres.

20 **Various food colourings** To create the icing colours used in the designs.

21 **Edible lustre** Snowflake and pink, to make cakes and decorations sparkle and shimmer.

22 **Edible glitters** Used as a highlight on rose petals and cupcakes.

23 **PME6 scriber needle** Used to score details onto cakes.

24 **Sharp knife or scalpel** For cutting straight edges or shapes precisely.

25 **Ruler** To help with levelling cakes and to measure sugarpaste strips.

26 **Florists' tape and wire in green and white** For fresh flower details and to wire up sugar flower displays.

27 **Card butterfly former** For creating a butterfly shape.

28 **Cake tins** Various shapes and sizes, mini heart and mini round tins.

29 **Sugar shaker** For decorative dusting on cakes, cookies and brownies.

30 **Rose leaf veiner** For giving texture to cut-out sugar rose leaves.

31 **PME blade and shell tool** For scoring lines and cutting into icing.

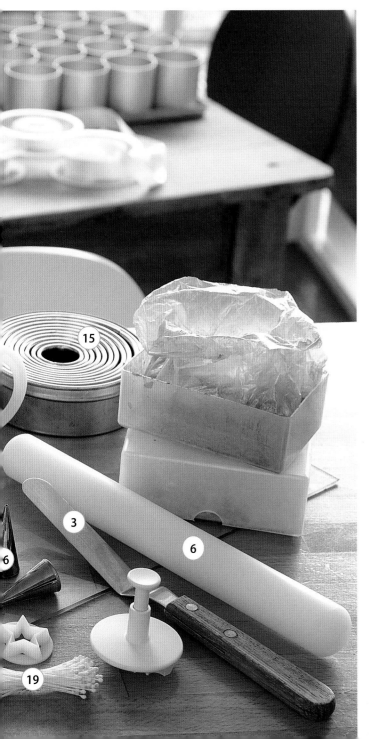

Preparation

To maximize your enjoyment of the whole cake-making process, always start with a clear workspace, with all the equipment and ingredients you need to hand. You will also have some time in between each step (while your cake cools, or your icing sets) to make flowers and to clean down your work surface in preparation for the next task.

Lining cake tins

A greaseproof lining is the best way to prevent the cake sticking to the bottom and sides of the cake tin. This is cut precisely to fit the tin and attached with melted butter or sunflower oil.

MATERIALS AND EQUIPMENT

- Cake tin
- Greaseproof paper
- Pencil
- Scissors
- Melted butter or sunflower oil
- Pastry brush

tip Try using a spray-on sunflower oil as a quick greasing method. This can be purchased from most well-stocked supermarkets.

one Lay out a sheet of greaseproof paper and place your cake tin on top. Draw around it with a pencil and cut out the circle or square (**a**).

two From the roll, cut a length of greaseproof paper 11cm (4½in) wide. Fold the length in half and in half again. Cut snips, about 2.5cm (1in) deep, along the bottom of the paper (**b**), then unfold.

three Melt some butter (or use sunflower oil) and brush it over the inside base and round the sides of the tin.

four Stick the length of greaseproof paper around the sides of the tin allowing the tabs to sit on the base (**c**). Place the cut-out circle or square on top, covering the tabs.

five If you are making a fruit cake, cover the outside of the tin with folded newspaper and tie on with string to prevent the outside from burning before the centre is cooked.

Cake Recipes and Charts

Here are the recipes for the cakes I like to make as the base for my designs. I've included charts so you can easily vary the quantities to make a larger or smaller version. And, of course, they're all perfect for cupcakes or mini cakes (see page 31).

Vanilla sponge cake

ROUND	15cm (6in)	18cm (7in)	20cm (8in)	22cm (9in)	25cm (10in)	28cm (11in)	30cm (12in)
SQUARE	12cm (5in)	15cm (6in)	18cm (7in)	20cm (8in)	22cm (9in)	25cm (10in)	28cm (11in)
Margarine/ softened butter	150g (5oz)	150g (5oz)	200g (7oz)	250g (9oz)	350g (12oz)	450g (1lb)	550g (1lb 4oz)
Caster sugar	150g (5oz)	150g (5oz)	200g (7oz)	250g (9oz)	350g (12oz)	450g (1lb)	550g (1lb 4oz)
Self-raising flour	150g (5oz)	150g (5oz)	200g (7oz)	250g (9oz)	350g (12oz)	450g (1lb)	550g (1lb 4oz)
Eggs	3	3	4	5	7	9	11
Vanilla extract	½ teaspoon	½ teaspoon	¾ teaspoon	1 teaspoon	1 teaspoon	1½ teaspoons	2 teaspoons
Baking time (approx)	50 mins	50 mins	50 mins	1 hr	1 hr 15 mins	1 hr 30 mins	1 hr 30 mins

Flavour variations

Quantities are for a 20cm (8in) round (four-egg) cake. You will need to modify them for a different sized cake.

Citrus – Add the zest of 1½–2 lemons or oranges to the mix (but NOT the juice).

Coffee – Add 50ml (2fl oz) espresso or concentrated instant coffee.

Banana – Add one very ripe mashed banana per egg.

Almond – Replace a quarter of the self-raising flour with an equal weight of ground almonds, two drops of almond extract and ½ teaspoon baking powder.

Method

one Preheat the oven to 160°C (315°F/ Gas Mark 2–3). Line the base of your tin only (see page 12) and grease the sides.

two Beat the margarine and sugar together until they are light and fluffy.

three Add the eggs one at a time, beating well after each addition.

four Sift in the flour and mix thoroughly.

five Add the vanilla extract.

six Pour the mixture into the tin, place in the oven and bake for the guide time listed in the recipe, or until the cake is lightly golden and a skewer inserted into the centre comes out clean.

seven Leave the cake to stand in the tin for five minutes before turning out onto a wire rack to cool.

Carrot cake

ROUND	15cm (6in)	18cm (7in)	20cm (8in)	22cm (9in)	25cm (10in)	28cm (11in)	30cm (12in)
SQUARE	12cm (5in)	15cm (6in)	18cm (7in)	20cm (8in)	22cm (9in)	25cm (10in)	28cm (11in)
Plain flour	170g (6oz)	250g (9oz)	440g (1lb)	500g (1lb 2oz)	750g (1lb 11oz)	875g (1lb 15oz)	1kg (2lb 3oz)
Soft brown sugar	120g (4oz)	175g (6oz)	300g (10½oz)	350g (12oz)	525g (1lb 3oz)	610g (1lb 6oz)	700g (1lb 9oz)
Caster sugar	120g (4oz)	175g (6oz)	300g (10½oz)	350g (12oz)	525g (1lb 3oz)	610g (1lb 6oz)	700g (1lb 9oz)
Sunflower oil	120ml (4fl oz)	165ml (5fl oz)	300ml (10fl oz)	350ml (12fl oz)	500ml (18fl oz)	610ml (20fl oz)	700ml (24fl oz)
Sour cream	40ml (1fl oz)	50ml (1½fl oz)	100ml (3fl oz)	120ml (4fl oz)	175ml (6fl oz)	210ml (7fl oz)	230ml (8fl oz)
Vanilla	1 teaspoon	2 teaspoons	3 teaspoons	4 teaspoons	6 teaspoons	7 teaspoons	8 teaspoons
Desiccated coconut	25g (1oz)	75g (3oz)	130g (4oz)	150g (5oz)	225g (8oz)	275g (10oz)	300g (11oz)
Bicarbonate of soda	½ teaspoon	1 teaspoon	1½ teaspoons	2 teaspoons	3 teaspoons	3½ teaspoons	4 teaspoons
Cinnamon	¾ teaspoon	2 teaspoons	3 teaspoons	4 teaspoons	6 teaspoons	7 teaspoons	8 teaspoons
Mixed spice	½ teaspoon	1 teaspoon	1½ teaspoons	2 teaspoons	3 teaspoons	3½ teaspoons	4 teaspoons
Salt	¼ teaspoon	½ teaspoon	¾ teaspoon	1 teaspoon	1½ teaspoons	1¾ teaspoons	2 teaspoons
Grated carrot	200g (7oz)	300g (11oz)	525g (1lb 3oz)	600g (1lb 5oz)	900g (2lb)	1050g (2lb 4oz)	1200g (2lb 10oz)
Orange zest	2	2	3	3	4	5	5
Eggs	2	3	5	6	9	11	12
Sultanas (soaked in brandy if desired!)	100g (3½oz)	150g (6oz)	200g (7oz)	250g (9oz)	300g (10½oz)	350g (12oz)	400g (14oz)
Rum or brandy	25ml (1fl oz)	35ml (1¼fl oz)	55ml (2fl oz)	65ml (2¼fl oz)	75ml (2¾fl oz)	90ml (3¼fl oz)	100ml (3½fl oz)
Baking time (approx)	1 hr 30 mins	1 hr 45 mins	2 hrs	2 hrs 15 mins	2 hrs 30 mins	2 hrs 45 mins	3 hrs

Method

one Preheat the oven to 160°C (315°F/Gas Mark 2–3).

two Line the cake tin, sides and base (see page 12).

three Mix the sunflower oil, sour cream, vanilla, eggs and orange zest together. Then add the two types of sugar.

four Into a separate bowl, sift the flour, spices, bicarbonate of soda and salt together.

five Combine the dry ingredients with the wet mixture.

six Add the grated carrot to the mixture along with the coconut and sultanas.

seven Bake for the guide time listed in the recipe or until a skewer inserted into the centre comes out clean.

eight Once out of the oven, leave the cake to cool in the tin.

tip For the deep cakes featured in the book, you will need two cakes of the same size to make a sandwich for the vanilla sponge recipe. The carrot, chocolate fudge and fruit cakes can be baked in one tin.

Traditional fruit cake

ROUND	15cm (6in)	18cm (7in)	20cm (8in)	22cm (9in)	25cm (10in)	28cm (11in)	30cm (12in)
SQUARE	12cm (5in)	15cm (6in)	18cm (7in)	20cm (8in)	22cm (9in)	25cm (10in)	28cm (11in)
Mixed fruit (sultanas, currants, raisins)	495g (1lb 2oz)	800g (1lb 12oz)	1000g (2lb 3oz)	1250g (2lb 12oz)	1590g (3lb 8oz)	1925g (4lb 4oz)	2350g (5lb 3oz)
Glacé cherries	25g (1oz)	50g (2oz)	75g (2½oz)	110g (4oz)	150g (5oz)	200g (7oz)	225g (8oz)
Mixed peel	25g (1oz)	50g (2oz)	75g (2½oz)	110g (4oz)	150g (5oz)	200g (7oz)	225g (8oz)
Oranges (zest and juice)	1	2	2	3	3	3	4
Softened butter	175g (6oz)	225g (8oz)	275g (10oz)	400g (14oz)	500g (1lb 2oz)	600g (1lb 5oz)	825g (1lb 13oz)
Dark brown sugar	175g (6oz)	225g (8oz)	275g (10oz)	400g (14oz)	500g (1lb 2oz)	600g (1lb 5oz)	825g (1lb 13oz)
Eggs	2	3	5	6	9	11	13
Plain flour	175g (6oz)	225g (8oz)	275g (10oz)	400g (14oz)	500g (1lb 2oz)	600g (1lb 5oz)	825g (1lb 13oz)
Cinnamon	1 teaspoon	1½ teaspoons	1½ teaspoons	2 teaspoons	2 teaspoons	2½ teaspoons	3 teaspoons
Mixed spice	1 teaspoon	1½ teaspoons	1½ teaspoons	2 teaspoons	2 teaspoons	2½ teaspoons	3 teaspoons
Brandy	8 tablespoons	10 tablespoons	12 tablespoons	14 tablespoons	16 tablespoons	18 tablespoons	20 tablespoons
Baking time (approx)	2 hrs 30 mins	3 hrs	3 hrs 15 mins	3 hrs 30 mins	3 hrs 30 mins	4 hrs 15 mins	5 hrs

Method

one Chop the cherries in half and place in a bowl with the mixed peel and the mixed fruit. Add the juice and zest of the oranges and half the quantity of brandy. Stir well. Leave overnight to soak.

two Preheat the oven to 150°C (300°F/ Gas Mark 2)

three Line the sides and bottom of your tin (see page 12). If it is larger than a 20cm (8in) round or 18cm (7in) square, wrap newspaper around the outside as well.

four Cream together the butter and sugar until they are thoroughly mixed.

five Add the eggs one at a time.

six Sift in the flour and the spices, then mix in the fruit mixture and stir well.

seven Transfer the cake mixture into your prepared tin, smooth the top of the mixture and place into the centre of the oven. Bake for the guide time listed in the recipe.

eight Once out of the oven, leave the cake to cool in the tin.

nine After baking, drizzle the cake with the remaining brandy.

ten Wrap the cake in cling film and store in an airtight container until required.

Chocolate fudge cake

ROUND	15cm (6in)	18cm (7in)	20cm (8in)	22cm (9in)	25cm (10in)	28cm (11in)	30cm (12in)
SQUARE	12cm (5in)	15cm (6in)	18cm (7in)	20cm (8in)	22cm (9in)	25cm (10in)	28cm (11in)
Margarine or butter	110g (4oz)	130g (4½oz)	190g (6½oz)	220g (8oz)	250g (9oz)	400g (14oz)	440g (15½oz)
Dark chocolate	110g (4oz)	130g (4½oz)	190g (6½oz)	220g (8oz)	250g (9oz)	400g (14oz)	440g (15½oz)
Instant coffee	2 teaspoons	3 teaspoons	4 teaspoons	6 teaspoons	8 teaspoons	12 teaspoons	2½ tablespoons
Water	80ml (2¾fl oz)	95ml (3fl oz)	140ml (5fl oz)	160ml (5½fl oz)	180ml (6fl oz)	290ml (10fl oz)	320ml (11fl oz)
Self-raising flour	65g (2oz)	75g (2½oz)	110g (4oz)	125g (4½oz)	150g (5oz)	250g (9oz)	280g (10oz)
Plain flour	65g (2oz)	75g (2½oz)	110g (4oz)	125g (4½oz)	150g (5oz)	250g (9oz)	280g (10oz)
Cocoa powder	25g (1oz)	30g (1oz)	40g (1½oz)	50g (1½oz)	60g (2oz)	90g (3oz)	110g (4oz)
Bicarbonate of soda	¼ teaspoon	¼ teaspoon	¼ teaspoon	½ teaspoon	½ teaspoon	¾ teaspoon	1 teaspoon
Caster sugar	240g (8½oz)	300g (10½oz)	420g (15oz)	480g (1lb 1oz)	550g (1lb 3oz)	860g (1lb 14oz)	960g (2lb 2oz)
Eggs	2	2	3	4	4	7	8
Vegetable oil	4 teaspoons	5 teaspoons	6 teaspoons	7 teaspoons	8 teaspoons	2½ tablespoons	3 tablespoons
Sour cream	60ml (2fl oz)	70ml (2½fl oz)	95ml (3fl oz)	110ml (3½fl oz)	125ml (4fl oz)	200ml (6½fl oz)	220ml (7fl oz)
Baking time (approx)	1 hr 5 mins	1 hr 20 mins	1 hr 30 mins	1 hr 40 mins	1 hr 45 mins	2 hrs 15 mins	2 hrs 30 mins

Method

one Preheat the oven to 160°C (315°F/ Gas Mark 2–3).

two Line the sides and base of the tin (see page 12).

three Gently melt the butter, chocolate, coffee and water in a pan on a low heat.

four Sift the dry ingredients (flours, cocoa and bicarbonate of soda) into a mixing bowl. Add the sugar.

five In a separate bowl, combine the eggs, oil and sour cream.

six Pour the egg mix and chocolate mix into the dry ingredients and stir well.

seven Pour into the cake tin and place in the centre of the oven.

eight Bake for the guide time listed in the recipe or until a skewer inserted into the centre comes out clean.

nine Remove from the oven and leave the cake to cool in its tin.

Portion guide

The size of your slice will determine how may portions you get out of a cake. These numbers are based on the depth of the cake multiplied by 2.5 x 5cm (1 x 2in) portions (approx).

Shape/Size	12cm (5in)	15cm (6in)	18cm (7in)	20cm (8in)	22cm (9in)	25cm (10in)	28cm (11in)	30cm (12in)
ROUND	6	12	17	22	28	38	47	56
SQUARE	12	18	24	32	40	50	55	72

These numbers are based on the depth of the cake multiplied by 2.5 x 2.5cm (1 x 1in) portions (approx).

Shape/Size	12cm (5in)	15cm (6in)	18cm (7in)	20cm (8in)	22cm (9in)	25cm (10in)	28cm (11in)	30cm (12in)
ROUND	12	23	32	44	56	67	84	100
SQUARE	25	36	49	64	81	100	111	144

Tin sizes

The depth of cake tin that I generally use is a 7.5cm (3in) or 10cm (4in) professional tin. If you are using a smaller tin, you may need to reduce the quantities of ingredients used.

tip If your cake tier is really deep, you may get more portions from it, so these numbers are just a guide – refer to each project for an estimate of how many it will serve.

Cup & US measurements

If you prefer to use cup measurements, please use the following conversions. (Note: 1 tablespoon = 15ml, except for Australian tablespoons which are 20ml):

butter
1 tablespoon = 15g (½oz)
2 tablespoons = 25g (1oz)
1 stick = 100g (3½oz)
1 cup = 225g (8oz)

caster (superfine) sugar
2 tablespoons = 25g (1oz)
1 cup = 200g (7oz)

soft brown sugar
1 cup = 115g (4oz)

liquid
1 cup = 250ml (9fl oz)
½ cup = 125ml (4fl oz)

flour
1 cup = 150g (5oz)

desiccated coconut (dry, unsweetened, shredded)
4 tablespoons = 25g (1oz)
1 cup = 75g (2½oz)

dried fruit
1 cup = 225g (8oz) currants, or 150g (5oz) raisins, or 175g (6oz) sultanas (golden raisins)

glacé (candied) cherries
1 cup = 225g (8oz)

Cake Fillings and Icings

A delicious filling makes a cake taste wonderful. Let the flavour of your cake help you decide what this should be, for example a cream cheese filling goes well with carrot cake and a classic buttercream and raspberry jam filling is perfect for a vanilla sponge. And then there is the icing. Here I describe the different types I use.

Buttercream

Buttercream is used to sandwich together two vanilla sponge cakes and to fill a chocolate or carrot cake.

MATERIALS AND EQUIPMENT

(For filling a three-tiered cake)

- 500g (1lb 2oz) salted butter
- 1kg (2lb 3oz) icing sugar
- 2 teaspoons vanilla extract
- Drop of milk (if needed)

Piping Cream
Buttercream can also be used as an icing (see Sunkissed Cupcakes, page 51).

one Cream the butter until the colour goes a little lighter.

two Sift the icing sugar and thoroughly mix with the butter.

three Add the vanilla extract and mix well. If the mixture is a bit too stiff, add a little milk to make a smooth consistency.

four Use on your cake following the steps for Levelling and Filling on page 21.

Additional fillings

There are lots of other fillings you can use as well as buttercream such as fruity jams and curds. For example, if you are making a lemon cake, try spreading a layer of lemon curd for the filling and make some lemon drizzle to go on top. I use Duchy Original Lemon Curd for a beautifully zesty flavour and pour caster sugar mixed with lemon juice over my sponge.

Buttercream variations

A traditional vanilla sponge is filled with simple buttercream and jam, but you can use chocolate or orange instead. Be creative and think about what flavours work well with each other. For example, a chocolate filling works equally well in an orange cake and an almond cake.

Add the following ingredients to flavour the basic buttercream recipe opposite:

Citrus – the rind and a little juice of 2–3 lemons or oranges.

Chocolate – 175g (6oz) melted plain chocolate.

Coffee – espresso or concentrated instant coffee, 5 tablespoons.

Cream cheese frosting – add equal amounts of cream cheese to buttercream, and lemon zest to taste.

Icing

There are three main types of icing I use to create my designs:

Sugarpaste

Also known as fondant icing, this soft pliable icing is used to cover cakes ready for decorating. When mixed with flowerpaste it becomes a good modelling icing.

Flowerpaste

This is used mainly for handmade sugar flowers but is ideal for any delicate sugarcraft work that requires the strength of a hard setting paste. It's perfect for flowers, bows and frills as it can be rolled out very thinly. It can be purchased from sugarcraft shops either in a small block or as a powder that is mixed with water.

Royal icing

Royal icing (shown left) is a wet mixture of egg whites (or albumen) and icing sugar that sets extremely hard. It's used for piping details such as flower centres or a snail trail onto cakes and also as a sugar glue for attaching decorations (see also page 26).

Preparing Cakes for Icing

There are a few handy cake-making techniques you need to know when getting your cake ready for icing. They will help you make every surface on your cake flat, smooth and level – a flawless blank canvas ready for you to create your design.

Covering cake boards

An iced cake board makes an excellent foundation for both single and multi-tiered cakes. It also provides another surface that can be incorporated into the design.

MATERIALS AND EQUIPMENT

- Thick cake board
- Sugarpaste (see right for quantities)
- Icing smoother
- Rolling pin
- Small sharp knife
- Small paintbrush

Quantity guide for covering cake boards (round or square)

Size of board	20cm (8in)	22cm (9in)	25cm (10in)	28cm (11in)	30cm (12in)	33cm (13in)	35.5cm (14in)	38cm (15in)	41cm (16in)
Approx quantity of sugarpaste	625g (1lb 6oz)	725g (1lb 9¾oz)	825g (1lb 13oz)	850g (1lb 14oz)	875g (1lb 15oz)	900g (2lb)	925g (2lb ½oz)	925g (2lb ½oz)	1kg (2lb 3oz)

a

b

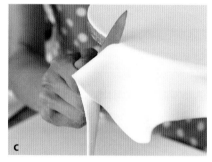

c

one Brush the cake board with a wet paintbrush, moistening the whole board without adding too much water.

two Roll out the sugarpaste about 3mm (¹⁄₁₆in) thick. Hold the board above the rolled-out icing to check that it will cover all of it.

three Roll the icing around the rolling pin, lift it up and lay it onto the wet cake board (**a**).

four Use the icing smoother to finish off, going over the board in a circular motion to leave a smooth surface (**b**).

five Holding the board in one hand, use the sharp knife to trim the excess sugarpaste all round, keeping the knife flush with the edge of the board (**c**).

six Allow the covered board to dry overnight before decorating it or placing the cake on it.

Levelling and filling

It's very important to make your cake level before you start decorating it, especially if you are adding tiers. For best results, use a small spirit level to check you've got it right rather than simply judging by eye.

one Work out what height your cake should be and mark it ready for trimming. Measure with a ruler to ensure it will be the same height all round (**a**).

two Trim the dome from the top of the cake using a sharp knife to make a flat surface (**b**).

three Place the cake on a board and spread with a generous layer of buttercream (see page 18) (**c**), then some jam if required. Gently place the second half of the cake on top, checking it is straight. If your sponges are deep, you may choose to add more layers of buttercream. Do this by cutting each of your sponges in half and adding three layers of the filling.

four Use a spirit level to check that the cake is flat. If it still needs levelling, add small amounts of sugarpaste icing (about the size of a small marble) under the cake to raise one side to the right level.

tip If you are worried about cake crumbs getting caught up in the buttercream, coat the cake in a really thin layer to start with and place it in the fridge to set. This will act as a seal, so you can add more buttercream without the risk of getting crumbs everywhere.

Icing Cakes

Applying two coats of icing to your cake will give a really smooth finish and provide the stability necessary for stacking tiers on top of each other. You can use different flavours for the under and top icing. For example, you can under ice a sponge cake in chocolate sugarpaste or marzipan like a fruitcake, if you wish. Again, the flavour of your cake will guide you.

Under icing

It's worth taking care over the under icing on your cake. The smoother the finish you can achieve at this stage, the easier it will be to add the top icing afterwards.

MATERIALS AND EQUIPMENT

- Cake
- Thin cake board the same size as the cake
- Palette knife
- Apricot glaze/seedless jam
- Icing sugar
- Pastry brush
- Sugarpaste (see opposite for quantities)
- Rolling pin
- Icing smoother
- Sharp knife

one Spread the cake with the glaze or jam (**a**) and set aside.

two Roll out the sugarpaste or marzipan about 5mm (⅛in) thick and large enough to cover the cake.

three Roll the icing around the rolling pin, lift up and lay onto the cake (**b**).

four Smooth the top and sides of the cake with your hands and an icing smoother to press the icing down onto the cake and form a cutting line (**c**).

five Trim the excess icing around the bottom of the cake with the sharp knife. Allow to dry overnight.

tip If you feel that the buttercream filling is too soft for you to ice the cake well, place the cake in the fridge for a little while to let the filling harden. This will give you a solid base on which to cover the cake.

Top icing

The top icing is added in the same way as the under icing, except that water is used instead of glaze. Allow yourself plenty of time to ensure you get a perfect finish.

a

b

one Place the under iced cake onto a board and brush with a little water. Moisten the whole cake without making it too wet.

two Dust a work surface with icing sugar, and knead the sugarpaste on it until smooth.

three Roll out the icing 5mm (⅛in) thick, large enough to cover the whole cake.

four Using the rolling pin, lay the icing over the cake as before.

five Smooth the top and the sides with your hands and an icing smoother (**a**).

six Trim the excess icing around the cake with a sharp knife (**b**).

seven If you see any air bubbles caught between the two layers of icing, carefully insert a clean pin to smooth the air out.

eight Use a little sugarpaste glue (water and sugarpaste mixed well) or royal icing to stick the cake onto an iced cake board (see page 20).

tip If you are an experienced cakemaker, you may prefer to use one coat of icing on a single tiered cake. The icing should be about 7mm (¼in) thick.

Quantity guides

Use these simple guides to calculate the quantity of sugarpaste and marzipan you will need when under icing and top icing your cake.

For under icing cakes

Size of cake (round or square)	15cm (6in)	18cm (7in)	20cm (8in)	22cm (9in)	25cm (10in)	28cm (11in)	30cm (12in)	33cm (13in)	35.5cm (14in)
Approx quantity of sugarpaste or marzipan	650g (1lb 7oz)	700g (1lb 8¾oz)	825g (1lb 13oz)	1kg (2lb 3oz)	1.25kg (2lb 12oz)	1.5 kg (3lb 5oz)	1.75kg (3lb 13¾oz)	2kg (4lb 6½oz)	2.5kg (5lb 8oz)

For top icing cakes

Size of cake (round or square)	15cm (6in)	18cm (7in)	20cm (8in)	22cm (9in)	25cm (10in)	28cm (11in)	30cm (12in)	33cm (13in)	35.5cm (14in)
Approx quantity of sugarpaste	750g (1lb 10oz)	900g (2lb)	1kg (2lb 3oz)	1.25kg (2lb 12oz)	1.75kg (3lb 13¾oz)	1.85kg (4lb 1¼oz)	2.25kg (4lb 15oz)	2.5kg (5lb 8oz)	3kg (6lb 10oz)

Assembling Tiered Cakes

There are various ways you can assemble the tiers on a cake, all of which include the use of dowels. These are made of plastic or wood and are specially designed to prevent each tier from sinking into the one underneath. Here is the method I prefer for my tiered designs.

Stacking cakes

In this technique, which is also known as American Style stacking, plastic cake-making dowels are pushed into the cake directly below where the next tier will go, enabling you to stack your tiers securely.

MATERIALS AND EQUIPMENT
(For a three-tiered cake)

- One 15cm (6in), one 20cm (8in) and one 25cm (10in) under and top iced cake tier, each mounted on a thin cake board the same size as the cake
- Iced thick cake board (see page 20)
- Royal icing (see page 26)
- 12 plastic dowels
- Small hacksaw or serrated knife
- Pencil
- Palette knife
- Scriber needle or pin

a

b

one Spread a small amount of royal icing onto the iced base board and place the largest tier centrally onto the board.

two Take a thin cake board, the same size as the next tier, and place it centrally on top of the bottom tier. Using a scriber needle or a pin, score the cake around the board (**a**). This helps you to position the dowels and tiers.

three Insert a dowel into the centre of this tier and make a mark on the dowel with a pencil or a knife to show the height of the cake (**b**).

four Remove the dowel and, using the hacksaw or knife, cut the dowel about 1mm (1⁄16in) above the marked line.

five Cut a further six dowels exactly the same size using the cut dowel as a measure (**c**). It's very important that all the dowels are the same size.

six Push the first dowel into the centre of the cake, then insert the six other dowels in a circle around it, staying inside the scored line (**d**).

seven Spread a small amount of royal icing on the centre of the cake. Using both hands, carefully place the next tier on top, using the scored line as a guide for positioning the cake board (**e**).

eight If you are making a three-tiered cake, repeat these steps with the top tier using five dowels this time.

Finishing Touches

Icing and ribbons can be used effectively to add that special finishing touch to your cake. Here I explain a few of my favourite techniques.

Royal icing

I use royal icing to create all of the delicate sugar pipe work and as a sugar glue to stick cake tiers together. Once made, the icing will last in an airtight container for up to seven days. You will only require a small amount of royal icing for each project.

Use one medium egg white (or the equivalent of reconsituted albumen powder) to 300g (10½oz) icing sugar. Beat together in a mixing bowl until smooth and the icing forms peaks. If the consistency is a little dry, add a few drops of lemon juice.

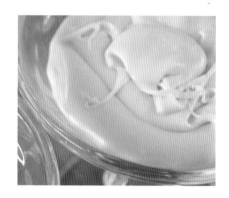

To make a piping bag for royal icing

a

b

c

one Fold some greaseproof paper about 33cm (13in) square in half to make a triangle and place on a table with the point facing you (**a**).

two Take the right-hand corner and fold around your hand to make a cone (**b**).

three Fold the left-hand corner all the way around the cone to meet the other side (**c**).

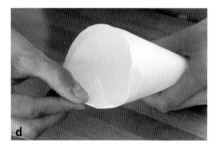

d

e

four Secure your piping bag by folding over the corner to the inside (**d**).

five Cut off the tip about 1cm (½in) from the end, and drop in your piping nozzle. You are now ready to pipe (**e**).

tip Avoid overfilling a piping bag in case it leaks from the top. Fill the bag no more than two-thirds full. Don't forget to add the nozzle first!

Snail trail

This pattern is usually piped along the line where the cake meets the cake board and is used on several of the cakes in this book – see Butterfly Bliss (page 74), Chocolate and Blue (page 94) and Frou-Frou Frills (page 108).

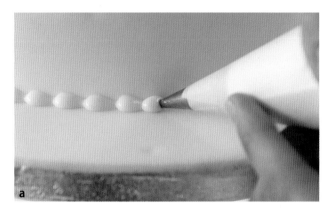

one Hold the piping bag at a 60-degree angle to your cake with the nozzle just touching the icing.

two Make a pearl of icing, and ease off the pressure as you move the piping bag to the right to make a tail. Pipe the next pearl over the tail of the previous pearl to make a continuous line (**a**).

three Continue all round the cake in this way, joining the last pearl neatly to the first one.

Using ribbon on cakes and boards

Instead of a snail trail you might choose to use a satin ribbon. This can often be a nice way of incorporating colour on a simply iced cake.

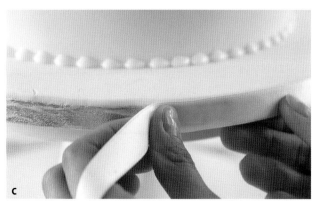

To ribbon a cake

one Cut your ribbon just slightly longer than the circumference of the cake. Wrap it round the base.

two With a little royal icing, stick one end of the ribbon to the cake, apply more icing to the upper side and stick the other end of the ribbon down on top (**b**).

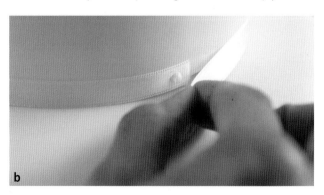

To ribbon a board

one Put the board onto a turntable and run all round the edge with a non-toxic glue stick.

two Without cutting the ribbon from the roll, stick the end to the board.

three Wind the ribbon all the way round the edge, sticking it down as you go (**c**).

four When you get back to the end, cut the ribbon, leaving a little extra to stick down on top.

Decorating cakes with fresh flowers

Fresh flowers look beautiful on a cake. They can be used to decorate a stacked or single-tiered cake. You could try matching them with the flowers that are being used in the bridal bouquet at a wedding or in the table setting at a party perhaps. Always remove fresh flowers before cutting and serving the cake, as they are not edible.

MATERIALS AND EQUIPMENT

- Posy picks
- Florists' tape
- Florists' wire
- Scissors

Garden Fresh
Make sure that your flowers are as fresh as possible. Collect the flowers from your florist on the day or the day before you need them.

one Gather a small posy of flowers, trim the ends and then bind the stalks with florists' tape (**a**).

two Place the display in a posy pick (**b**) and insert into the cake. If your display is a little larger, you can use a little florists' wire to hold the display together.

Cupcakes and Mini Cakes

Cupcakes really are a favourite any-time treat for kids, big and little! They are so simple to create, take no time to bake and cool in minutes. I often make more mixture than I need to for a large cake so I can include some sneaky cupcakes for tea. Mini cakes take a little longer, but can be a real showstopper. They're perfect for a very special occasion.

Cupcakes

Any of the recipes on pages 13–16 (except for the fruit cake) work perfectly as cupcakes, especially the chocolate fudge cake and carrot cake which are both very moist. You will get around 12 cupcakes from an 18cm (7in) round recipe.

MATERIALS AND EQUIPMENT

- Muffin tin
- Muffin cases
- Wire cooling rack

one Preheat the oven to 160°C (315°F/ Gas Mark 2–3). Line a muffin tin with muffin cases.

two Make your cake mixture using your chosen recipe from pages 13–16. Fill each muffin case about two-thirds full. Bake for around 20 minutes until they bounce back on touch.

three Leave to cool for a few minutes and then turn out onto a wire rack.

four There are several ways to finish the cupcakes – you can pipe buttercream onto each cake with a savoy star-shaped nozzle or smooth it on and add a circle of rolled-out sugarpaste, then decorate as desired.

Mini cakes

You can make mini cakes either with individual mini cake tins or by baking a slab cake about 5cm (2in) deep and cutting out rounds with a 5cm (2in) pastry cutter (this method leaves plenty of leftover cake to sample!). Individual tins are best for ensuring your mini cakes are all the same size and height. Mini cake tins are available in a variety of shapes including round, square and heart-shaped.

Any of the recipes on pages 13–16 are suitable for mini cakes. Grease the individual tins well and fill each one about two-thirds full. You will get 25 mini cakes from a 30cm (12in) square tin recipe.

Icing mini cakes

Iced mini cakes really do look special. They are iced in the same way as a larger cake but only need a single coat. Festive mini cakes can be under iced with marzipan.

MATERIALS AND EQUIPMENT
- Sugarpaste, 2.5kg (5lb 8oz) for 25 mini cakes
- Apricot glaze or seedless jam
- Rolling pin
- Icing smoother

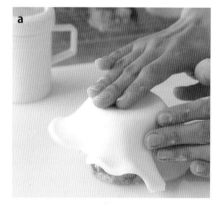

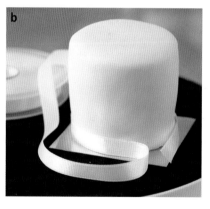

one When the cakes are cooled, cut each one in half and fill with buttercream and jam as required (see page 18).

two Brush each mini cake with apricot glaze or seedless jam.

three Roll out the icing about 5mm (⅛in) thick and cut a 14cm (5½in) square for each cake.

four Place a square over each cake and smooth down with your hands and an icing smoother (**a**). Trim the excess with a sharp knife and set on a tray lined with greaseproof paper.

five Allow the mini cakes to harden for a couple of hours. Cut a length of satin ribbon to fit around each cake and attach with a little royal icing (see page 27) (**b**).

Cookies

Cookies are quick and easy to make and are a great way to continue the theme of a larger cake. A few cookies tied up with ribbon or placed in a cellophane bag make great take-home treats either for children's parties or as wedding favours.

Butter cookies

This is my tried-and-tested recipe for delicious cookies. They can be plain or delicately flavoured (see box) and iced or just dusted with sugar.

MATERIALS

- 175g (6oz) butter
- 200g (7oz) caster sugar
- 2 large eggs
- 400g (14oz) plain flour (plus extra for dusting)
- 1 teaspoon baking powder
- Golden granulated sugar (optional – see tip)

EQUIPMENT

- Electric mixer with paddle attachment
- Sieve
- Cling film
- Large rolling pin
- Cookie cutters
- Baking tray
- Small palette knife
- Wire cooling rack

Cookie flavourings

The cookies can be flavoured in several different ways. Add the following ingredients to the basic recipe:

Vanilla – add 1 teaspoon of pure vanilla extract.

Lemon – add the zest of one lemon.

Orange – add the zest of one orange.

Chocolate – replace 50g (2oz) of the plain flour with organic cocoa powder.

tip If you are not going to ice and decorate the cookies, sprinkle them with a little golden granulated sugar for a crunchy texture when baked.

one Preheat the oven to 180°C (360°F/Gas Mark 4). Cream the butter and sugar together in an electric mixer until pale and creamy, then beat in the eggs until well combined.

two Sift in the plain flour, baking powder and chosen flavouring and mix on a low speed until the dough forms. If you feel the dough is a little too sticky, add a tiny amount of flour.

three Half the dough, form into balls, wrap in cling film and chill in the fridge for at least an hour to make the dough easier to work with.

four Place one ball of dough on a floured surface (**a**), sprinkle a little extra flour on top of the dough and roll out to about 0.5cm (¼in) thick.

five Using your chosen cutters, cut out the cookie shapes (**b**). Repeat steps four and five with the second ball of dough.

six Place the cookies onto a greased baking tray (**c**) and bake in the centre of the oven for 12–15 minutes until golden brown.

seven When cooked, remove the tray from the oven and use a palette knife to lift the cookies onto a wire rack to cool completely (**d**).

Icing cookies

There are a number of ways to decorate a cookie, some simpler than others. You could just dust them with a little icing sugar or cocoa powder, or you can cover them with rolled-out sugarpaste or royal icing.

Sugarpaste icing

This technique gives you an immediate flat, dry surface onto which you can then add further decorations if desired. This is a soft icing that doesn't set hard.

one Roll out the sugarpaste to a thickness of approximately 3mm (⅛in) and cut out a shape using the same cutter that was used to make your cookies (**a**).

two To help the sugarpaste to stick, brush the cookie with a little seedless jam, lemon curd or icing sugar mixed with water, depending on the flavour of your cookie.

three Carefully place the sugarpaste shape onto the cookie (**b**) and smooth the edges of the icing with your fingertips.

Royal icing

This method creates cookies that have a hard, crispy coating when dry. When the icing is still wet, decorate the cookies with piped sugar pearls, sugar flowers or silver balls to complement the main cake design.

one Mix a little royal icing to a soft peak consistency (see page 26). Fill a piping bag with a no.1.5 nozzle and the icing. Pipe a steady outline around each cookie shape (**a**).

two Mix some further royal icing with some lemon juice or water to a runny consistency. Place the icing in a piping bag, snip the tip off the end of the bag and flood the centres of the cookies with icing (**b**).

three Use a small paintbrush to brush the icing up to the piped outline, being careful not to let the icing overflow around the edges (**c**).

Sweet
Nothings

Forget-me-not

The Forget-me-not has been my favourite flower ever since I can remember, and their evocative, romantic name makes them all the more appealing. They grew in abundance in the garden of my childhood home and I wanted to capture the beauty of these tiny blossoms with this exquisite design. This cake is ideal to share with your loved ones at a special gathering.

a

one Dowel the bottom tier and stack the cakes (see pages 24–25). Fix the pale pink satin ribbon around the base of each tier with a little royal icing. Make sure that the joins line up at the back of the cakes.

two Mix a little ice blue food colouring and a tiny amount of grape violet with the white flowerpaste to make the Forget-me-not blue. Roll out the icing about 1mm (1/16in) think and cover it with a stay-fresh plastic mat so that it doesn't dry out.

three Cut out the small flowers using the plunger cutter and form them on the flower foam pad (**a**). Make approximately 20 flowers for each cluster of flowers. For a 12cm (5in) and 20cm (8in) round cake you will need 12 clusters of flowers.

SERVES
About 50

MATERIALS
- One 12cm (5in) and one 20cm (8in) round white iced cake, each set onto a round cake board the same size as the cake
- 2.5cm (1in) pale pink satin ribbon
- White flowerpaste, 150g (5oz)
- White royal icing (see page 26)
- Food colouring: ice blue, grape violet, spruce green and melon yellow

EQUIPMENT
- No.1.5 icing nozzle
- Leaf icing nozzle
- Piping bags
- Small blossom plunger cutter
- Stay-fresh plastic mat
- Flower foam pad
- Scriber needle or pin
- Small paintbrush
- Rolling pin
- Five plastic dowels

The Forget-me-nots are so simple to create and their delicate colour stands out beautifully against the white icing.

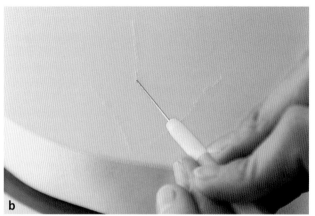

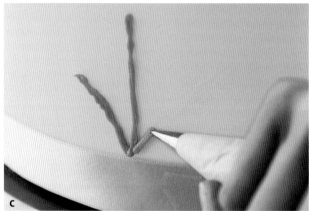

four Using a scriber needle or pin, score the side of the cake with three lines for the flowers stems (**b**). Repeat around both the cakes, spacing them so that you have seven stems on the large cake and five on the smaller cake.

five Mix some royal icing with some spruce green and a little melon yellow food colouring for the leaves and stems. Fill a piping bag with a leaf nozzle and the green icing.

six Pipe down the scored lines on the cake (**c**) and add little leaves to the stems. Dab down any icing peaks with a little water.

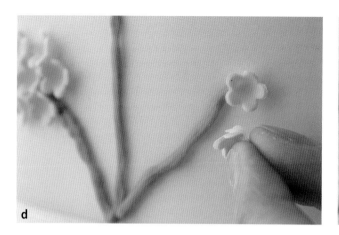

seven Fill a piping bag with a no.1.5 nozzle and some white royal icing. Stick the small flowers to the cake using a little of this icing (**d**).

eight With the same piping bag, pipe small sugar pearls around the top of the satin ribbon and pipe the centres of the flowers with a tiny dot (**e**). Dab down any icing peaks with a little water.

nine Take a small amount of melon yellow food colouring and place in a small dish. Add a little water and use this to paint the centres of the flowers (**f**).

tip An eggcup is the perfect size to mix the food colouring in.

Simply Irresistible

These are the most delicate and pretty cookies – perfect for a springtime wedding when soft pastel shades are everywhere.

Unforgettable Cookies

one Bake round butter cookies in two sizes (see pages 34–35). If you want to add a hole to attach a ribbon for hanging, make it with a drinking straw or a small circle cutter before they go into the oven.

two Ice the cookies in white sugarpaste (see page 36). If you are hanging them, cut a corresponding hole in the icing to allow a ribbon to slip through.

three Decorate the cookies with Forget-me-nots. The larger size of cookie is perfect for adding a cluster, very similar to the cake (see steps two to seven, pages 41–43). The smaller cookies look very sweet dotted with single blooms and leaves. Finish with a circle of piped white sugar pearls.

On Display

Hanging the cookies from a whitewashed branch makes a beautiful table centrepiece. Pretty pink ribbon is all you need to complete the look. If you want a double-sided effect, stick two cookies together back to back with a few spots of royal icing after you've decorated them.

Summer Sun

For this cake, I wanted to design something really bright and fun. The vibrant pink flowers set off the sunny yellow cake beautifully. Violet is classically the complementary colour for yellow, but I felt that this pink just adds a little more merriment! It would be perfect for a summer wedding or garden party.

a

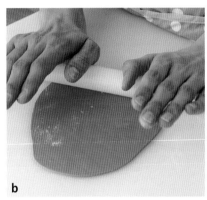

b

one Dowel and stack the cakes (see pages 24–25) using six dowels on the bottom tier and four on the middle tier.

two Mix around 100g (3½oz) of white flowerpaste with some pink food colouring to make a deep pink shade (**a**).

three Roll out the icing about 2mm (¹⁄₁₆in) thick (**b**) and use a sharp knife to cut out 45 strips measuring 1.5cm (½in) wide by 9cm (3½in) long.

SERVES
About 70

MATERIALS
- One 15cm (6in), one 18cm (7in) and one 22cm (9in) round yellow iced cake, each set onto a cake board the same size as the cake
- 2.5cm (1in) ivory satin ribbon
- White flowerpaste, 125g (4½oz)
- Food colouring: pink and spruce green

EQUIPMENT
- No.2 icing nozzle
- Piping bag
- Small leaf cutter or medium daisy cutter
- Ruler
- Sharp knife
- PME blade and shell tool (or similar blade tool)
- Stay-fresh plastic mat
- Flower foam pad
- Small paintbrush
- Small rolling pin
- Double-sided tape
- Ten plastic dowels

c

d

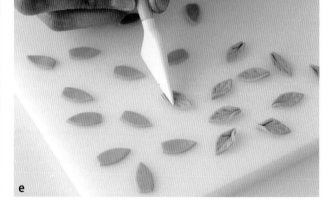

e

four Take one strip of icing and brush a little water onto one side. Fold the top over and roll the folded strip up creating little pleats as you go (**c**). Pinch the excess icing off the bottom and set aside to dry. Repeat to make 45 flowers in total.

tip Place the icing strips under a stay-fresh plastic mat until you need them so they don't dry out.

five Mix around 25g (1oz) of white flowerpaste with some spruce green food colouring. Roll out the icing about 1mm (1/16in) thick and cut out small leaves, or use a daisy cutter as I have done and cut off the petals (**d**). You will need 45 leaves, one per flower.

six Place the leaves onto the flower foam pad and score a line and vein details down the centre of each leaf with a blade tool. Pinch the end of each leaf to give it more of a 3D shape (**e**). Set aside to dry.

seven Mix up some yellow icing leftover from covering the cake with some water to make a paste with a royal icing consistency (**f**). Fill a piping bag with a no.2 nozzle and the yellow icing.

eight Fix the ivory satin ribbon around the base of each tier with a little of the yellow icing. With more of the yellow icing, stick on the flowers and leaves evenly spaced all over the cake, positioning the leaves at different angles (**g**).

nine Finish the design with a bow made from the ivory satin ribbon; attach this to the base of the middle tier using double-sided tape.

Bright and Breezy

I just love the cheery feel this cake has. The colour scheme has such summery connotations. I defy any of your guests not to feel uplifted by a slice of this!

Simply Irresistible

The flowers from the Summer Sun cake and pink candy balls are used to adorn these delicious bite-sized chocolate cupcakes, covered with chocolate-orange buttercream.

Sunkissed Cupcakes

one Bake some chocolate cupcakes following the instructions on page 31.

two Fill a piping bag with a savoy star-shaped nozzle and some chocolate-orange buttercream (see pages 18–19) and pipe the top of each cupcake.

three Decorate the top of some of the cupcakes with flowers and leaves made in the same way as the main cake (see steps two to six, pages 47–48) but making some flowers in violet as well as pink. Push some pink candy balls (available from confectionary shops and cake-decorating suppliers) into the tops of other cupcakes for some visual variety and a bit of crunch!

Perfect Piping
Using a savoy star-shaped icing nozzle is a simple way to create a great effect. Start from the outside of the cake and pipe inwards round in a circle until you reach the centre.

Rose and Daisy

This pretty single-tiered cake is decorated with lovely open sugar roses, small violet blossoms and daisies – perfect for an intimate summer garden wedding. The colours of the flowers and the ribbon around the base of the cake can be changed to match the colour scheme of the wedding.

a

SERVES
About 30

MATERIALS
- One 18cm (7in) round white iced cake, set onto a round cake board the same size as the cake
- 1.5cm (½in) ivory ribbon
- White flowerpaste, 175g (6oz)
- White sugarpaste, 50g (2oz)
- White royal icing (see page 26)
- Food colouring: pink, grape violet and spruce green
- Snowflake lustre dust
- Spaghetti

EQUIPMENT
- No.1.5 icing nozzle
- Piping bag
- Rose petal cutters, one large, one small
- Medium daisy cutter
- Small primrose cutter
- Rose leaf cutter
- Small heart plunger cutter
- Flower foam pad
- Stay-fresh plastic mat
- Bone tool
- Rose leaf veiner
- Painter's palette
- Small paintbrush
- Rolling pin
- Dusting brush
- Double-sided tape

one For this cake you will need approximately ten roses. You will need the make the roses a few days in advance as they need to be left to dry – preferably overnight – at each stage. Mix around 50g (2oz) of white flowerpaste with the same quantity of white sugarpaste. Add enough pink food colouring to the icing to make a soft rose colour.

two With a little ball of the pink icing, make a cone shape that is just a little shorter than your small rose petal cutter. Dip a short length of spaghetti into some water and insert it into the bottom of the cone. Allow to dry overnight (**a**).

three For the next stage of the sugar rose, roll out the pink icing about 1mm (1⁄16in) thick. Cut out the small petal shapes and place them under a stay-fresh plastic mat. When you are ready to use them, curl them three at a time with a bone tool on the flower foam pad.

four Brush the cone with a little water and wrap the first petal around it tightly so that the tip is completely covered. Take another two petals and repeat this process, curling the edges out with your fingertips (**b**). Apply a further three petals, curling out the edges. Leave to dry overnight.

five When the roses are completely dry, you can continue to add more large petals. Add five petals at a time and allow to dry. Each rose requires approximately 15 petals. While you are waiting for the roses to dry, you can get on with making the other sugar flowers and leaves.

six Roll out 50g (2oz) of white flowerpaste to about 1mm (1⁄16in) thick. With a medium daisy cutter, cut out 14 flowers. On a flower foam pad, curl the petals towards you using a bone tool. Put a dab of water in the centre of one flower then stick another flower on top, ensuring the petals are not overlapping (**c**). Place the seven completed flowers into a painter's palette to dry overnight.

seven Take 25g (1oz) of white flowerpaste and add a small amount of grape violet food colouring. Roll out the icing about 1mm (1⁄16in) thick and cut out around 15 small flowers with the primrose cutter. Again, shape the petals on the flower foam pad using the small end of your bone tool. Leave these to dry for at least two hours (**d**).

eight To make the leaves, mix a little spruce green food colouring with 25g (1oz) of white flowerpaste. Roll out the icing about 1mm (1⁄16in) thick and cut out the leaf shapes with a rose leaf cutter. You will need around ten leaves.

Beautiful Blooms

The soft pink, lilac and green shades of the flowers and foliage give a wonderfully fresh feel to this cake. For a more passionate theme, try using bolder shades.

nine Press each leaf into the rose leaf veiner and then curl the very edges of the leaves on the flower foam pad with the small end of the bone tool (**e**). Allow to dry for a few hours.

ten Roll a golf-ball sized ball of sugarpaste (leftover from covering the cake), flatten it a little and place it on the top of the cake. Fill a piping bag with the no.1.5 nozzle and some white royal icing and use this to secure the roses and daisies around the ball (**f**).

eleven When the roses and daisies are in place, attach the violet flowers and leaves to fill any gaps in the arrangement and dust the flowers with snowflake lustre dust.

twelve Fix the ivory ribbon around the base of the cake with a little royal icing. Attach a ribbon bow to the base of the cake with some double-sided tape.

thirteen Roll out 25g (1oz) of white flowerpaste about 1mm (1⁄16in) thick, and cut out little hearts using the heart plunger cutter. Stick these around the top of the ribbon using a little water. Use the same piping bag and nozzle as in step ten to pipe tiny pearls in between the hearts (**g**). Dab down any icing peaks with a little water.

fourteen Using the same piping bag, pipe small pearls into the centres of the daisies and small blossom flowers and trailing down onto the top of the cake. Dab down any icing peaks with a little water.

The hearts and sugar pearls around the base of the cake are beautifully understated, giving the design a sophisticated finishing touch.

Simply Irresistible

Creating a flat surface on a cupcake means that you can have fun with colours and intricate design details. These cupcakes are iced in a complementary soft greeny-blue and finished off with little flowers, leaves and sugar pearls to match the main cake.

Floral Fancies

one Bake some cupcakes and cover them with buttercream following the instructions on page 31.

two Mix some white sugarpaste with eucalyptus food colouring to make a soft shade. Ice the cupcakes with a circle of the rolled-out icing.

three Decorate the tops of the cakes with different arrangements of violets, daisies and leaves as used on the cake (see steps six to nine, pages 54–56). For efficiency, make the extra flowers and leaves you need for the cupcakes at the same time as you make the ones for the main cake.

four Finish the designs by piping a circle of white sugar pearls around the edge of each cake and some extra sugar pearls around the flowers, then sprinkle with some edible glitter.

Cookie Stack

An elegant stack of butter cookies (see pages 34–35) tied up with matching ribbon makes a perfect take-home treat for your guests. Rather than icing them, just dust them with golden granulated sugar before baking them for a delicious crunchy texture.

Raspberry Ripple

I couldn't resist including this delicious cake. No sugarcraft techniques are required, but structure and precision play a big part in making this cake look extra special. The effects of the dusted icing sugar, fresh fruit and flowers create a very beautiful cake that is just mouth-watering!

a

SERVES
About 65

MATERIALS

- Two 10cm (4in), two 18cm (7in) and two 25cm (10in) vanilla sponge cakes (see page 13)
- One 8cm (3in), one 15cm (6in) and one 22cm (9in) thin cake board
- Vanilla buttercream (see page 18)
- Raspberry jam
- Fresh strawberries and raspberries, 550g (1lb 3½oz)
- 12 fresh red and pink roses
- Icing sugar

EQUIPMENT

- Long sharp knife
- Ruler
- Sugar shaker
- Florists' tape or posy pick
- 11 plastic dowels

one Using a long sharp knife, cut each of your sponge cake layers 4cm (1½in) deep and cut each of these in half so you have four layers of sponge at 2cm (¾in) deep for each tier (**a**).

two Carefully fill each layer with some vanilla buttercream followed by some raspberry jam, being careful that the jam does not spill over the sides of the cake (**b**).

three Place the 10cm (4in) cake onto the 8cm (3in) board, the 18cm (7in) cake onto the 15cm (6in) board and the 25cm (10in) cake onto the 22cm (9in) board.

four Insert six dowels into the bottom tier, following the instructions for stacking cakes on pages 24–25. Place the middle tier on top of the bottom tier and repeat the process with the top tier using five dowels (**c**).

five Generously dust the whole cake with icing sugar using the sugar shaker.

six When you are ready to serve the cake, place it on a cake stand or plate and decorate it with the fresh fruit and flowers as shown (see also pages 28–29).

Fruity Flavour

I've chosen vanilla buttercream with raspberry jam, but you could use strawberry or cherry jam, or even lemon curd. They will all taste delicious.

Simply Irresistible

When I found these delightful little heart-shaped tins, I instantly thought they would work perfectly as mini dusted jam and cream sponges. Sweet, simple and delicious!

Queen of Hearts

one Bake some heart-shaped mini cakes with a vanilla sponge recipe (see pages 13 and 33).

two Cut each cake in half and fill with vanilla buttercream (see page 18) and raspberry jam.

three Dust generously with icing sugar using a sugar shaker.

Jammy Dodgers
You've got to love these! Roll out some butter cookie dough then cut out two circles for each cookie. Cut a small heart out of one of the circles and spoon jam onto the other. Place the circle with the cut-out heart on top of the jam and bake (see pages 34–35 for cookie recipe).

Look
of Love

Shooting Star

I love stars and have done ever since I was a little girl. I painted them everywhere and would often receive star-themed presents. The brooch used on this cake was one such gift and seemed a perfect theme for a sophisticated cake design.

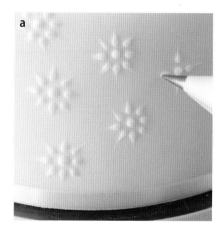

a

one Dowel and stack the cakes (see pages 24–25) using seven dowels for the bottom tier (six in a circle and one in the centre) and four for the middle tier.

two Fill a piping bag with a no.1.5 nozzle and some white royal icing. Fix a length of white satin ribbon around the base of each tier and secure with the royal icing.

three To create the starbursts on the top and bottom tiers, first pipe a small sugar pearl onto the side of the cake. Then pipe eight slightly smaller pearls around it; pipe the first, then pipe the second opposite it, then repeat the process, always piping the next pearl opposite the previous one to ensure equal spacing. Pipe the pearl and drag the nozzle away from the centre to create the teardrop effect (**a**). Dab down any icing peaks with a little water.

SERVES

About 60

MATERIALS

- One 12cm (5in), one 18cm (7in) and one 22cm (9in) round white iced cake, each set onto a round cake board the same size as the cake
- 1cm (⅜in) white satin ribbon
- 1cm (⅜in) grey satin ribbon
- White royal icing (see page 26)
- Silver star brooch
- White disco hologram edible glitter

EQUIPMENT

- No.1.5 icing nozzle
- Piping bag
- Small paintbrush
- Double-sided tape
- 11 plastic dowels

Be Inspired

An exquisite brooch was the inspiration for this cake. If you have your own favourite brooch or piece of jewellery, why not use it as the basis for one of your own designs?

four Fix two lengths of grey satin ribbon around the base of the middle tier with some royal icing. Pipe little sugar pearls around the middle tier, dabbing down any icing peaks with a little water.

five Once the icing has dried, brush a little edible glitter onto the central pearl of each starburst on the top and bottom tiers (**b**).

six Cut three lengths of the grey satin ribbon about 75cm (30in) long and tie all three together in one go to make the bow. Attach the bow to the side of the cake with some double-sided tape and then pin the brooch to the centre of the bow.

b

tip To get the edible glitter to stick, you may need to brush the pearls with a little water first.

Starry Eyed

Position the starbursts evenly across the top and bottom tiers for a pleasing effect. With all the starbursts in place the design really starts to come to life.

The understated design of this cake is complemented by the flamboyant triple bow with its sparkly brooch adornment.

Simply Irresistible

Simple and sparkly, these white iced cookies are little showstoppers. Sprinkled with white edible glitter, they really are simply irresistible!

Twinkling Stars

one Bake some star-shaped butter cookies (see page 34–35).

two Ice the cookies with royal icing, following the instructions on page 37.

three While the icing is still wet sprinkle the cookies with white edible glitter. Sparkle-tastic!

Butterfly Bliss

A truly romantic cake, this beautiful butterfly design marries the elegance of classic 18th-century Wedgwood designs with the modern whimsy of butterflies and bows. Using the white relief designs, this cake would work in other colours to match a wedding or anniversary theme, perhaps chocolate brown or soft yellow.

a

b

one Mix up some blue icing leftover from covering the cakes and cake boards with a little water to make a paste with a royal icing consistency. Fill a piping bag with a no.3 nozzle and the blue icing and pipe a snail trail around the base of each cake (see page 27).

two Roll out around 100g (3½oz) of white flowerpaste about 1mm (¹⁄₁₆in) thick. Cut out around 14 large butterflies

and use the small blossom plunger cutter to cut patterns in the butterfly wings (**a**). Keep the blossom flowers to use on the cake. Cut out around 25 small butterflies. Cover the butterflies and the flowers with a stay-fresh plastic mat so that they don't dry out.

three Cut out a further nine large butterfly shapes and place in a card butterfly former (**b**).

SERVES
About 80

MATERIALS
- One 15cm (6in), one 20cm (8in) and one 25cm (10in) round pale blue iced cake, each set onto a round pale blue iced cake board 2.5cm (1in) larger than the cake (see pages 20–23)
- One 33cm (13in) round pale blue iced cake board (see page 20)
- Two 15cm (6in) round cake boards
- 2.5cm (1in) ivory satin ribbon
- 1.5cm (⅝in) ivory satin ribbon
- White flowerpaste, 200g (7oz)
- White sugarpaste, 100g (3½oz)
- White royal icing (see page 26)
- Glue stick

EQUIPMENT
- No.3 icing nozzle
- Piping bags
- Butterfly cutters, one large, one small
- Small blossom plunger cutter
- Stay-fresh plastic mat
- Card butterfly former
- Ruler
- Sharp knife
- Small paintbrush
- Rolling pin
- Nine plastic dowels

four Using a little water and a small paintbrush, stick the butterflies and blossom flowers to the sides of the top and bottom tiers in a pleasing arrangement (**c**). Don't forget to leave space for your 3D fluttering butterflies.

five Fill a piping bag with a no.3 nozzle and some white royal icing. Pipe down the centre of each butterfly to form the body, and from the top of each butterfly pipe the antennae. Pipe a dot into the centre of each blossom flower (**d**).

Winged Dimension
The 3D butterflies are simple to apply and add movement to the airy, light feel of this design.

e

f

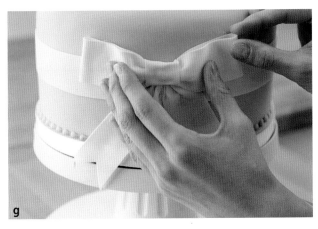

g

tip I find using a ruler for cutting the width of the ribbon is ideal, as you can just cut on either side of the ruler's edge (e).

six When the 3D fluttering butterflies are dry, stick them to the sides of the cake using a little royal icing. Pipe the bodies and antennae as before.

seven Mix 100g (3½oz) of white flowerpaste with the same quantity of white sugarpaste to make the bow on the middle tier.

eight Roll out the icing in a long thin strip and cut out two lengths 33cm (13in) long by 3.5cm (1¼in) wide (or the ruler's width – see tip, above right) (**e**). Stick these two lengths around the centre of the middle tier with a little water to create a ribbon band. Make sure that any joins in the band are at the front and back of the cake.

nine Cut out four more strips 13cm (5in) long by 3.5cm (1¼in) wide) and one smaller strip 5cm (2in) long.

ten Form the bow. Cut an inverted V shape in the end of two lengths to make the 'tassle' end and pinch the tops together. Fold

the other two lengths in half and pinch the ends together as shown. Place the two loops together and wrap the small length of icing around them and stick with a little water (**f**).

eleven Stick the bow tassles to the middle of the cake with a little water, covering up the ribbon band join, in an inverted V shape. Using a little royal icing, secure the bow onto the side of the cake (**g**).

twelve Place a 15cm (6in) board on the top-middle of the 20cm (8in) and 25cm (10in) cake. Score around the boards and then dowel and stack the cakes (see pages 24–25) using five dowels in the bottom tier and four in the middle tier.

thirteen Stick the two 15cm (6in) cake boards together with a little glue and edge with the 2.5cm (1in) ivory satin ribbon. Place on top of the 25cm (10in) cake as a separator between the bottom and middle tiers. Use the 1.5cm (⅝in) ivory satin ribbon to edge the other four boards, securing with glue (see page 27).

Simply Irresistible

There is something sumptuous and decadent about chocolate cupcakes,
and these swirling, butterfly-topped treats are sure to delight your guests.

Butterfly Kisses

one Roll out some white flowerpaste about 1mm (¹⁄₁₆in) thick. Cut out the butterflies using a small butterfly cutter and form in a card former (see step three, page 75).

two Bake some chocolate cupcakes following the instructions on page 31.

three Fill a piping bag with a savoy star-shaped nozzle and some chocolate buttercream (see pages 18–19). Pipe the top of each cupcake, starting on the outside and working round in a circle until you reach the centre.

four Gently push a butterfly into the top of each cake.

Create a Theme
Look out for pretty cupcake cases, like these lacy butterfly ones. They can make even the simplest cakes look amazing, and tying them in with your theme results in a professional designer look.

Ivory Swag

This cake is a simple expression of elegance and style. Delicate sugar swags are draped around the cake like necklaces and the gold painted sugar pearls add a touch of glamour and opulence. The top tier is finished with a passionate posy of sugar roses.

a

one You will need to make the roses a few days in advance. Follow steps one to five on pages 53–54 but using lilac food colouring instead of pink (**a**). This design requires about 11 roses, so the quantity of sugarpaste and flowerpaste needed has been increased accordingly.

two Dowel and stack the cakes (see pages 24–25) using nine dowels in the bottom tier, seven in the next tier and four in the final tier. Fix the gold ribbon around the base of each tier with a little royal icing and the ivory satin ribbon around the large cake board with some glue (see page 27).

SERVES

About 100

MATERIALS

- One 10cm (4in), one 15cm (6in) and one 20cm (8in) round ivory iced cake, each set onto a round cake board the same size as the cake
- One 28cm (11in) round ivory iced cake, set onto a 36cm (14in) round ivory iced cake board (see pages 20–23)
- 1cm (⅜in) gold ribbon
- 1.5cm (½in) ivory satin ribbon
- White sugarpaste, 75g (2½oz)
- White flowerpaste, 75g (2½oz)
- White royal icing (see page 26)
- Gold edible paint
- Food colouring: lilac
- Snowflake lustre dust
- Spaghetti
- Glue stick

EQUIPMENT

- No.2 icing nozzle
- Piping bag
- Rose petal cutters, one large, one small
- Bone tool
- Flower foam pad
- Stay-fresh plastic mat
- Ruler
- Small paintbrush
- Dusting brush
- Rolling pin
- 20 plastic dowels

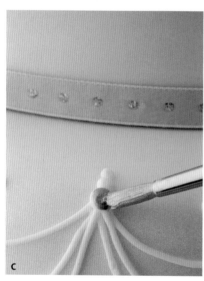

three Fill a piping bag with a no.2 nozzle and some white royal icing. Pipe small sugar pearls around the top of the first tier approximately 5cm (2in) apart using a ruler to get the height the same each time. Dab down any icing peaks with a little water.

four Once you have piped all the dots, slightly tilt your turntable away from you then pipe the swags dot to dot. Finishing off the design with three small sugar pearls at the bottom of each swag and a little loop on the top of the sugar pearl (**b**).

five On the bottom and middle tiers of the cake, create more swags by piping dot to dot again but making multiple swags at different heights.

six Finish off the designs on the bottom and middle tiers by piping two dots above the sugar pearls and adding a further sugar pearl in between the swags around the top of the cake.

seven Using gold edible paint on a small paintbrush, paint only the sugar pearls that the sugar swags are attached to (**c**).

eight Stick a small ball of ivory sugarpaste (leftover from covering the cakes) on the top tier and arrange the sugar roses around it, securing with a little royal icing. Place seven roses around the ball of icing and place the further four on the top to fill in any gaps, nestling the roses into the ball of icing (**d**). Finally, dust the sugar roses with some snowflake lustre dust.

Simply Irresistible

The piped swag motif works with a wide range of colours so whatever your colour scheme, this design will be a hit. These mini cakes are a great way to make the main cake go further – the lovely lilac icing with just a touch of gold gives a nice regal feel.

Mini Lilac Swags

one Bake some mini cakes, ice them in lilac sugarpaste and edge each cake with ivory satin ribbon, following the instructions on page 33.

two Pipe the swag and pearl design onto each cake and paint the pearls with gold edible paint (see steps three to seven, page 82).

three Place a white sugar flower (made in the same way as in the Chocolate and Blue cake, page 95) on top of each cake to complete the design.

Rosebud Ripples

Cute cupcakes make a simpler alternative to the mini cakes. Bake up a batch of chocolate cupcakes (see page 31), then pipe the tops with a savoy star-shaped nozzle and chocolate buttercream (see pages 18–19). Shake on some chocolate sprinkles and then push one of the roses from the main cake into the top of each cupcake.

Polka-Dot Chic

These little sweeties pay small homage to Audrey Hepburn in the 1964 musical *My Fair Lady* – the black-and-white polka-dot ribbon and the pink flowers are a gesture to one of her fabulous costumes. The uniformity of the ribbon and flowers makes this cake very chic!

MATERIALS

- Ivory iced round mini cakes (see page 33)
- One 15cm (6in) round ivory iced cake, set onto an 18cm (7in) round ivory iced cake board (see pages 20–23)
- 1.5cm (½in) polka-dot satin ribbon
- White flowerpaste, 100g (3½oz)
- White royal icing (see page 26)
- Pink lustre dust
- Ten fresh daisies (to decorate the top tier)
- Glue stick

EQUIPMENT

- No.1.5 icing nozzle
- Piping bag
- Daisy cutters, one small, one large
- Bone tool
- Small rolling pin
- Flower foam pad
- Stay-fresh plastic mat
- Dusting brush
- Small paintbrush

one Roll out the white flowerpaste about 1mm (1⁄16in) thick and brush lightly with some pink lustre dust with an uneven coverage (**a**), then cover with a stay-fresh plastic mat to stop it drying out.

two Cut out one large and one small daisy for each flower. You will need three flowers per mini cake and 15 flowers for the top tier. Curl the petals on a flower foam pad using the small end of your bone tool (**b**).

three Stick a small daisy on top of a large daisy using the small paintbrush and a little water. Set aside to dry for a couple of hours (**c**).

four Fill a piping bag with the no.1.5 nozzle and some white royal icing. Edge all the mini cakes and the top tier with the polka-dot satin ribbon, securing at the back with a little royal icing. Fix a length of ribbon around the cake board with glue (see page 27).

five Stick three flowers to the sides of each of the mini cakes using a little royal icing (**d**).

six Pipe the centres of the flowers and nine small sugar pearls around the cluster of flowers (**e**). Dab down any icing peaks with a little water.

seven Decorate the top tier with four little clusters of three flowers and the same sugar pearl design. Dress the top with the fresh daisies (see pages 28–29).

Choosing the polka-dot ribbon makes these pretty daisy cakes a little more retro and fun. The design has a sweet, girly feel that your guests will love.

Simply Irresistible

These lovely matching daisy cookies would be perfect served alongside the cake as an alternative to a mini cake or an extra treat for your guests. You could think about placing them in a bag and tying them with the same polka-dot ribbon.

Divine Daisies

one Bake some daisy-shaped butter cookies (see pages 34–35).

two Roll out some white sugarpaste and cut out daisy shapes using the same cutter as for the cookies. Ice the cookies (see page 36) and then dust with pink lustre dust.

three Pipe the centres of the flowers with some white royal icing and dust with pink lustre dust.

Young
Love

Chocolate and Blue

I adore the decadence of a chocolate iced cake. The little chocolate pearls and blue flowers on this design add a contemporary touch and the ribbons around the cakes are edible. You can change the colours of the flowers, but soft pastel shades work best with the rich chocolate colour.

one You will need to make the blue flowers a day or two in advance so that they can set. Mix the flowerpaste and sugarpaste together and add a little baby blue food colouring to make a soft pale blue shade.

two Roll out the blue icing about 1mm (¹⁄₁₆in) thick and cut out three large and three small flowers.

three Shape the petals on all of the flowers using a bone tool and flower foam pad (**a**).

four Place the large flowers into shallow bowls and insert the smaller flowers inside the large flowers, sticking with a little water. Leave them to set (**b**).

tip To prevent the flowers from sticking, shake a little icing sugar into the bottom of each bowl.

MATERIALS
- One 12cm (5in) round chocolate-brown iced cake, set onto a cake board the same size as the cake
- One 20cm (8in) round chocolate-brown iced cake, set onto a 28cm (11in) round chocolate-brown iced cake board (see pages 20–23)
- 1.5cm (½in) brown satin ribbon
- White flowerpaste, 50g (2oz)
- White sugarpaste, 50g (2oz)
- Food colouring: baby blue
- Glue stick

EQUIPMENT
- No.1.5 icing nozzle
- Piping bag
- Flower cutters, one small, one large
- Small blossom plunger cutter
- Bone tool
- Flower foam pad
- Stay-fresh plastic mat
- Ruler
- Three shallow bowls
- Sharp knife
- Small paintbrush
- Rolling pin
- Four plastic dowels

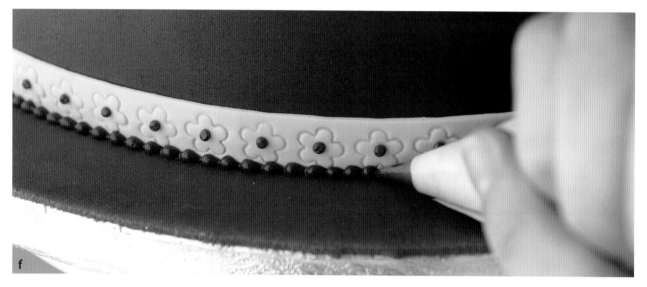

five Dowel and stack the cakes (see pages 24–25) then fix the brown ribbon around the cake board with glue (see page 27).

six Roll out the remaining blue icing into a long and thin shape. With a sharp knife, cut out a few strips of icing about 1cm (⅜in) wide by 16cm (6¼in) long (**c**). Place the rest of the rolled-out icing under a stay-fresh plastic mat, as you might need more strips later.

seven Indent the strips of icing using the small plunger blossom cutter (**d**).

eight Brush a little water around the bottom of each tier and carefully stick the strips of icing to the cakes (**e**).

nine Mix up a little of the chocolate-brown sugarpaste (leftover from covering the cakes) with some water to create a smooth, slightly runny icing. Fill a piping bag with the no.1.5 nozzle and the brown icing.

ten Pipe little dots into the centres of the indented blossom flowers and pipe a small snail trail (see page 27) around the top and bottom of the blue strip (**f**).

eleven Pipe small dots evening spaced over the whole cake (**g**). Dab down any icing peaks with a little water.

twelve Pipe little dots into the centres of the sugar flowers leaving the small sugar peaks to give the centres some texture (**h**).

thirteen Once the flowers are set, stick them to the sides of the cake as shown, using a little of the brown icing in the piping bag.

Perfect Petals

The sugarpaste and flowerpaste mix for the petals must be rolled out very thinly to ensure they look delicate. Curl the petals in different directions for a realistic effect.

Simply Irresistible

These little temptations are delicious and simple to make. Once the circles have been cut out, there is plenty of brownie leftover to enjoy with a cup of tea when you've finished the hard work! They are perfect boxed as wedding favours or as a dessert served with a little fruit coulis and ice cream. The quantities given below create four.

Mini Brownie Wedding Cakes

one Preheat the oven to 160°C (315°F/Gas Mark 2–3). Line a 20cm (8in) square baking tin with some greaseproof paper (see page 12).

two Cut 185g (6½oz) unsalted butter into small pieces and place in a heatproof glass bowl. Break 185g (6½oz) dark chocolate into the butter. Place the bowl over a pan of boiling water, ensuring that the bottom of the bowl isn't touching the water. On a low heat, stir the chocolate and butter until mixed and melted. Let the mixture cool to room temperature.

three Sieve 85g (3oz) plain flour and 40g (1½oz) cocoa powder into a bowl and set aside. Break three large eggs into another bowl and pour in 275g (10oz) golden caster sugar. Using an electric whisk, cream the eggs and sugar together until they are thick and creamy.

four Pour the cooled chocolate mix over the egg and sugar mix and really gently fold together with a spatula so you don't knock out the air. Fold until the mixture is a mottled dark brown.

| tip Creaming the eggs and sugar together can take up to eight minutes. The mixture needs to go pale and double its original volume.

five Resift the flour and cocoa powder mix into the chocolate mix. Fold until the mixture is fudgy, again being as gentle as you can to keep in the air.

six Pour the mixture into the prepared tin and ease it into each corner. Bake for 25–30 minutes (see tip below). The top should be shiny and the side should be just coming away from the tin. Leave in the tin until completely cold.

tip Remove the brownie from the oven after 25 minutes. If it wobbles in the middle, place it back into the oven for a further 5 minutes.

seven Remove from the tin and gently cut out three circles for each cake with 6.5cm (2½in), 4.5cm (1¾in) and 2.25cm (⁷⁄₈in) round cutters (**a**).

eight Level off each circle of brownie with a sharp knife and assemble the tiers, securing with a little extra melted chocolate.

nine Fill a piping bag with a no.1.5 nozzle and some white royal icing and decorate some of the cakes with little sugar pearls and swags (**b**). Dust others with icing sugar (refer to picture on previous page).

Chocolate Hearts

As an extra touch, heart-shaped chocolate butter cookies (see pages 34–35) can be sandwiched together with melted chocolate and then dusted with cocoa powder to make some utterly adorable wedding favours.

Paris in Spring

I designed this cake when I found the beautiful cake stand. It reminded me of the antique white metal scroll furniture seen in French gardens. Iced in soft colours and decorated with little sugar daisies and fresh roses, this cake would be wonderful for a spring garden wedding.

a

b

one Roll out the white flowerpaste to about 1mm (⅟₁₆in) and cut out around 50 small daisies. Curl the petals on a flower foam pad with the small end of a bone tool. Put a little dab of water in the centre of one daisy and stick another daisy on top, ensuring that the petals are not overlapping. Allow the 25 completed flowers to dry for a couple of hours.

two Fill a piping bag with a no.2 nozzle and some white royal icing. Pipe a dot into the centres of the daisies (**a**) and dab down any icing peaks with a little water.

three Take the 20cm (8in) board and place it on top of the 25cm (10in) cake. Check the board is centred then score around it using a scriber needle or pin (**b**). Repeat this process using the 15cm (6in) board on the 20cm (8in) cake and the 10cm (4in) board on the 15cm (6in) cake.

tip If you don't have the right sized cake board to score around, use a plate or saucer instead. As long as the plate is roughly 5cm (2in) smaller than the cake it will be fine.

SERVES
About 80

MATERIALS
- One 15cm (6in), one 20cm (8in) and one 25cm (10in) round shell-pink iced cake, each set onto a round cake board the same size as the cake
- One 10cm (4in), one 15cm (6in) and one 20cm (8in) cake board (to score around)
- Wilton 'Graceful Tiers' cake stand
- 2.5cm (1in) sage green satin ribbon
- White flowerpaste, 25g (1oz)
- White royal icing (see page 26)
- Food colouring: melon yellow
- Nine fresh roses with a little foliage (for decoration)

EQUIPMENT
- No.2 icing nozzle
- Piping bag
- Small daisy cutter
- Flower foam pad
- Scriber needle or pin
- Bone tool
- Ruler
- Small paintbrush
- Rolling pin

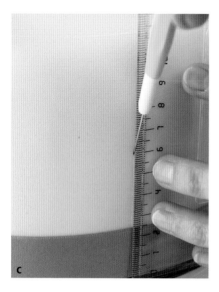

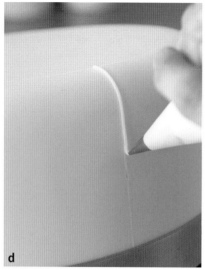

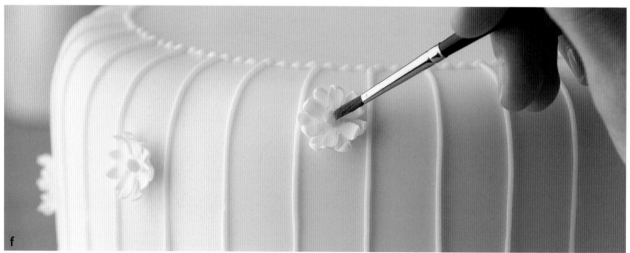

four Fix the sage green satin ribbon around the base of each cake with a little royal icing.

five Using a ruler as a guide, score a vertical line up the side of each cake, starting at the top of the ribbon and ending at the scored line on top of the cake (**c**).

six Using the same nozzle and piping bag used for the daisy centres, pipe a vertical line along the scored line from the top of each cake to the top of the ribbon around the base (**d**).

seven Using the first piped line as a guide pipe vertical lines around the sides of each cake approximately 2.5cm (1in) apart. Use your ruler each time to ensure a straight line if you need to.

eight When you have finished the vertical lines. Pipe a small snail trail (see page 27) around the scored line on top of each cake (**e**).

nine Attach the daisies with a little royal icing and paint the centres of the flowers using the melon yellow food colouring mixed with a little water (**f**).

ten Pipe three small dots around the top of the ribbon, in between the vertical piped lines on each cake. Dab down any icing peaks with a little water.

eleven When you are ready to present the cake, set it onto the cake stand and dress if with a few fresh roses (see pages 28–29).

Using fresh flowers on a cake is a lovely way to incorporate the floral theme at your celebration into the cake design so that everything is beautifully coordinated.

Simply Irresistible

Matching mini cakes presented in clear plastic gift boxes make a perfect present for special guests, such as bridesmaids and groomsmen to say thank you for all their help.

Petits Parisians

one Make and ice your mini cakes following the instructions on page 33 and fix a length of sage green satin ribbon around the base of each cake with a little royal icing.

two Use the same technique as in the main cake to score and then pipe the design onto the cakes (see steps five to eight, page 104).

three Stick three daisies from the main cake on the top of each mini cake using a little royal icing. Place into clear plastic gift boxes and finish with another length of ribbon and a sprig of fresh foliage.

Daisy Favours
Small butter cookies (see pages 34–35) decorated with simple daisies and small sugar pearls can be placed into cellophane bags to make wedding favours to complement the cake. Tie up the bags with a length of coordinating ribbon and add a small fresh flower as a finishing touch.

Frou-Frou Frills

I was so delighted with this cake and the cupcakes and cookies to match. I adore the different designs on each tier and the large sugar flowers in matching colours are so frilly and fun. Mini polka dots, pin stripes, hearts and flowers and pink: I love everything about this cake!

a

b

SERVES
About 70

MATERIALS
- One 12cm (5in), one 18cm (7in) and one 25cm (10in) round ivory iced cake, each set onto a round cake board the same size as the cake
- 1cm (⅜in) brown satin ribbon
- White sugarpaste, 150g (5oz)
- White flowerpaste, 300g (10½oz)
- White royal icing (see page 26)
- Food colouring: brown and pink

EQUIPMENT
- Two No.2 icing nozzles
- No.3 icing nozzle
- Piping bags
- Small circle cutter or drinking straw
- Small heart cutter
- Rose petal cutters: 4cm (1½in) and 3cm (1¼in)
- Small rolling pin
- Stay-fresh plastic mat
- Supermarket apple tray
- Polystyrene or kitchen paper
- Flower foam pad
- Bone tool
- Scriber needle or pin
- Small paintbrush
- Ruler
- Ten plastic dowels

one Start by making the sugar flowers. You will need five flowers, three pink and two brown. Divide the white flowerpaste and mix two-thirds with pink food colouring and one-third with brown. Roll out both colours about 2mm (1/16in) thick (**a**). Cover the icing with a stay-fresh plastic mat so that it doesn't dry out.

two For each flower, cut out 13 petals – nine large and four smaller ones. Place the petals on the flower foam pad and feather the edges with the bone tool (**b**).

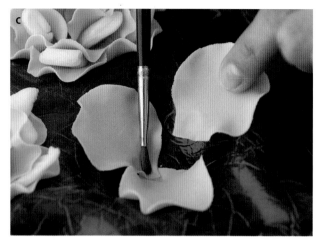

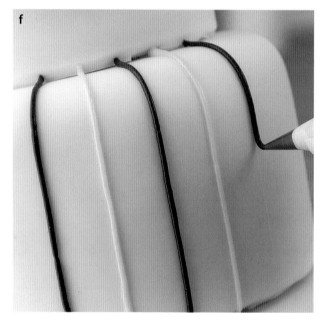

three Wet the petals with the paintbrush and a little water and arrange them on top of each other in a rose shape. A supermarket apple tray makes an ideal base for this (**c**).

four Place a piece of polystyrene or rolled up kitchen paper between each of the petals and leave to harden overnight (**d**).

five Dowel and stack the cakes (see pages 24–25) using six dowels in the bottom tier and four in the middle tier.

six Mix up some royal icing with pink food colouring and some more with brown food colouring (**e**). Fill two piping bags with no.2 piping nozzles and the pink and brown icing.

seven Using your ruler as a guide, take a scriber needle or pin and score a vertical line down the side of the middle tier, from the base of the top tier all the way down to the bottom of the cake.

eight Tilt your turntable away from you slightly and pipe a vertical line down the side of the cake using the scored line as a guide.

nine Using the first line as a guide, pipe vertical lines around the side of the cake about 2.5cm (1in) apart, using your ruler each time to ensure a straight line if you need to. Alternate between the pink and brown icing (**f**).

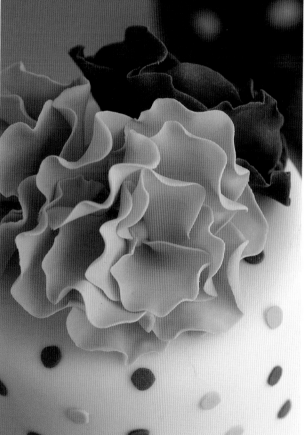

ten Fill a piping bag with a no.3 nozzle and some white royal icing. Pipe a snail trail (see page 27) around the base of the top and middle tiers.

eleven Divide the white sugarpaste and mix half with pink food colouring and half with brown. Roll out both colours about 2mm (¹⁄₁₆in) thick and cut out hearts and polka dots using a small circle cutter or a drinking straw (**g**).

twelve Brush a little water onto the polka dots and hearts and stick them to the sides of the top and bottom tiers (**h**). Edge the bottom tier with the brown satin ribbon and secure at the back with a little royal icing.

thirteen Carefully remove the polystyrene from the sugar flowers. Arrange three flowers (two pink and one brown) on the top tier around a little ball of ivory sugarpaste leftover from covering the cake, and stick two flowers (one of each colour) to the side of the bottom tier.

Flowery Flourish

The frilly sugar flowers on top of this cake are what make it so extra special, so take your time when making them to ensure that the petals are nicely arranged. The flowers give this cake its frou-frou appeal, so need to be just right!

Simply Irresistible

Because of the different designs on each tier of the main cake and the great colour combinations, it's easy to create some really special variations for this cake.

French Fancies

one Make some chocolate cupcakes following the instructions on page 31.

two Smooth the cupcakes with chocolate buttercream (see pages 18–19) and then ice with a circle of rolled-out ivory, pink or chocolate sugarpaste.

three Decorate with different combinations of sugarpaste hearts and mini polka dots, and piped pin stripes.

Dotty Heart Cookies

Make some heart-shaped butter cookies (see pages 34–35) of different sizes and use pink and chocolate sugarpaste and royal icing to decorate them (see pages 36–37) The little button cookies are small circle cookies decorated with a pink or brown chocolate button, which can be purchased from most confectionary shops, secured with a little coloured icing.

Love Heart

Love is in the air! Beautiful deep red sugar roses and pretty pipework ensure this bold cake is a showstopper at any celebration, while the clean, graphic lines will appeal to even the most modern romantic. Present this to a loved one in your life, whether it's for your sweetheart at an engagement party, or simply to show a friend how much you care.

a

b

SERVES
About 25

MATERIALS

- One 20cm (8in) round ivory iced cake set onto a round cake board the same size as the cake
- 2.5cm (1in) purple satin ribbon
- White flowerpaste, 100g (3½oz)
- White sugarpaste, 75g (2½oz)
- White royal icing (see page 26)
- Food colouring: red and spruce green

EQUIPMENT

- No.1.5 icing nozzle
- Piping bag
- Small star or calyx cutter
- PME blade and shell tool (or similar blade tool)
- Scriber needle or pin
- Tracing paper
- Thin card
- Small paintbrush
- Rolling pin

one Mix around 75g (2½oz) of flowerpaste with the same quantity of sugarpaste. Add enough red food colouring to turn the mixture a deep red.

two To make the roses, shape small balls of red icing and flatten them out with your fingers to make petals, keeping the edges neat. You will need five petals per rose. Take a petal and curl it around to create the centre of the rose. Wrap four further petals around the centre bud to form your rose (**a**). You will need 20 roses for this design. If you have any red icing leftover, make a few extra roses to decorate the plate.

three Mix some spruce green food colouring with around 25g (1oz) of white flowerpaste and roll out about 2mm (1⁄16in) thick. Cut out a star shape to make a calyx for each rose. With a blade tool, cut the bottom off each rose so they are about 2cm (¾in) high (**b**). Stick on the calyx with a little water and a paintbrush.

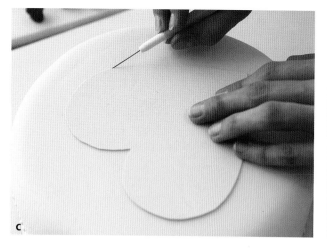

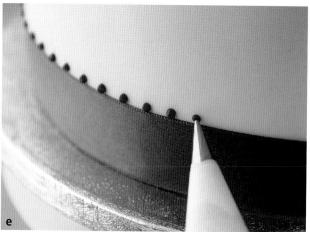

four Copy the heart template on page 121 onto tracing paper. Transfer the image onto a piece of thin card and cut it out. Place in the centre of your cake and score around the edge with a scriber needle or pin (**c**).

five Using a little white royal icing, stick your roses along the scored heart line on top of the cake (**d**).

six Edge the cake with the purple satin ribbon. Then mix up some royal icing with red food colouring. Fill a piping bag with the no.1.5 nozzle and the red icing. Pipe small dots evenly spaced around the top of the ribbon (**e**). Dab down any icing peaks with a little water.

tip If you are unsure how to pipe the dots at an equal height around the cake, pipe your first dot then use a ruler to measure its position from the bottom of the cake. Use this measurement as your guide.

seven Pipe dots around the top edge of the cake about 2.5cm (1in) apart.

eight Slightly tilt your turntable away from you, then pipe swags dot to dot, finishing off the design with a small piped heart (**f**). Pipe another row of hearts in the same way, about 2.5cm (1in) apart around the side of the cake.

Simply Irresistible

What could be cuter than these little heart-shaped cookies? The bold outline of the cookies perfectly complements the graphic red-on-white design. They are the ideal gift for a special valentine.

Budding Romance

one Bake heart-shaped butter cookies and ice them in ivory sugarpaste (see pages 34–36).

two Make the rosebuds (see steps one to three, page 115) and stick one onto the centre of each cookie with a little royal icing.

three Decorate the cookies with different designs to ensure they look interesting when grouped together. Experiment with adding small piped sugar pearls and outlines and leaving some white with just the rosebud.

All Wrapped Up
With such a bold design, these little cuties only need a clear bag and red satin ribbon to create modern gifts or favours.

Suppliers

UK

Maisie Fantaisie
Tel: 020 8671 5858
www.maisiefantaisie.co.uk
For new recipes sign up to May's blog at www.maisiefantaisie.co.uk/blog

For general sugarcraft materials:

Knightsbridge PME Ltd
Chadwell Heath Lane
Romford
Essex
RN6 4NP
Tel: 020 8590 5959
www.cakedecoration.co.uk

Squires Kitchen
Squires House
3 Waverley Lane
Farnham
Surrey
GU9 8BB
Tel: 0845 22 55 671
www.squires-group.co.uk

Surbiton Art and Sugarcraft
140 Hook Road
Surbiton
Surrey
KT6 5BZ
Tel: 020 8391 4664
www.surbitonart.co.uk

The Bakers Boutique
020 8333 1559
www.thebakersboutique.com
info@thebakersboutique.com

For ribbons:

John Lewis
Haberdashery Department
www.johnlewis.com for nearest
store finder

V V Rouleaux
54 Sloane Square
London
SW1W 8AX
Tel: 020 7730 3125
www.vvrouleaux.com

For floristry:

Mathew Dickinson
Cabin J
25 Horsell Road
London
N5 1XJ
Tel: 020 7503 0456
www.mathewdickinsonflowers.com

US

Pfeil and Holing
58–15 Northern Boulevard
Woodside
NY 11377
Tel: (718) 545-4600 / (800) 247-7955
www.cakedeco.com

New York Cake Supplies
56 West 22nd Street
New York
NY 10010
Tel: (800) 942-2539 / (212) 675-2253
www.nycake.com

Sweet Celebrations
PO Box 39426
Edina
MN 55436
Tel: (800) 328-6722
www.sweetc.com

About the Author

May Clee-Cadman founded Maisie Fantaisie in 2003 to create unique wedding and celebration cakes. She studied Art and Design History graduating with an honours degree in 2000, and went on to train as a cake designer, incorporating her flair for design with her love of cake making.

Acknowledgments

I had such a great response from readers of my last book, *Sweet and Simple Party Cakes*, expressing their delight at the designs and saying that I inspired them to get out their rolling pins and aprons and bake! It made the process of making this second book exciting and challenging, as I knew I had to create something wonderful and new for my readers. My first thanks, therefore, go to all the people who have sent me emails and cards expressing their joy at my first book. For *Sweet and Simple Romantic Cakes*, I would like to thank my sister Isa for all of her help and support, and the team at David & Charles, in particular Sarah Underhill and Ame Verso. A big thank you also goes to my photographer, Ginette Chapman, it was a pleasure working with you again. And Daron, thank you for everything – this one's for you.

Index

Heart Template — *see page 116*